A TRIP TO THE FARM

DAIRY FARMS

URSULA PANG

PowerKiDS press

New York

Published in 2023 by The Rosen Publishing Group, Inc.
29 East 21st Street, New York, NY 10010

First Edition

Editor: Greg Roza
Designer: Leslie Taylor

Photo Credits: Cover Anton Havelaar/Shutterstock.com; series artwork (background) OHishiapply/Shutterstock.com; p. 5 Jenoche/Shutterstock.com; p. 7 (Holstein) VanderWolf Images/Shutterstock.com; p. 7 (Jersey) Joe Gough /Shutterstock.com; p. 9 fotopanorama360/Shutterstock.com; p. 11 Ben Schonewille/Shutterstock.com; p. 13 HQuality/Shutterstock.com; p. 15 Zyabich/Shutterstock.com; p. 17 Photoagriculture/Shutterstock.com; p. 19 Lucky Business/Shutterstock.com; p. 21 Pavel L Photo and Video/Shutterstock.com.

Cataloging-in-Publication Data

Names: Pang, Ursula.
Title: Dairy farms / Ursula Pang.
Description: New York : Powerkids Press, 2023. | Series: A trip to the farm | Includes glossary and index.
Identifiers: ISBN 9781725339453 (pbk.) | ISBN 9781725339477 (library bound) | ISBN 9781725339460 (6pack) | ISBN 9781725339484 (ebook)
Subjects: LCSH: Dairy farming–Juvenile literature. | Dairy farms–Juvenile literature.
Classification: LCC SF239.5 P364 2023 | DDC 636.2'142–dc23

Manufactured in the United States of America

CONTENTS

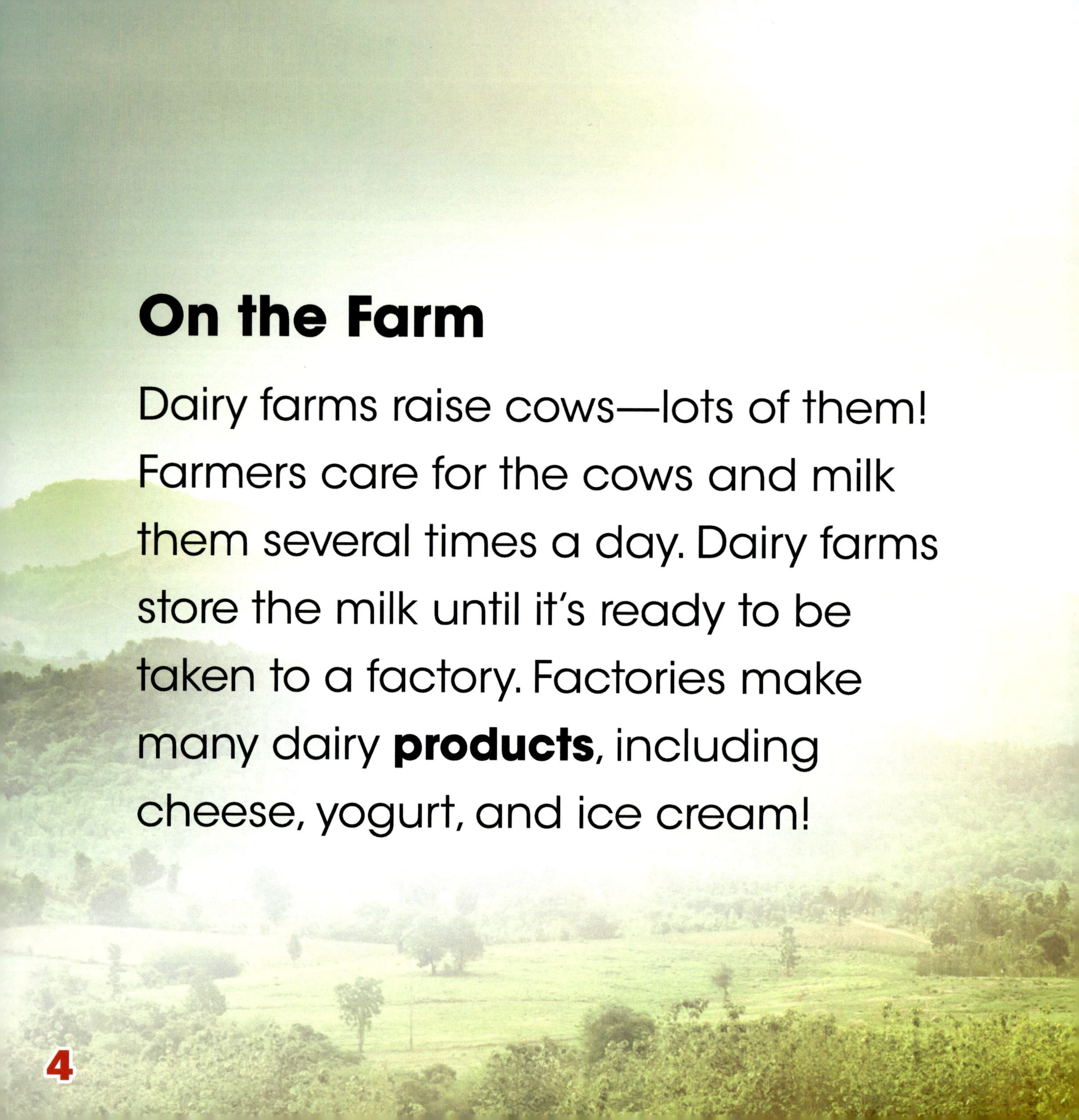

On the Farm

Dairy farms raise cows—lots of them! Farmers care for the cows and milk them several times a day. Dairy farms store the milk until it's ready to be taken to a factory. Factories make many dairy **products**, including cheese, yogurt, and ice cream!

Cow Breeds

Many cow **breeds** are raised for their milk. The most common breeds are Holsteins and Jerseys. Cows aren't the only animals raised on dairy farms. People also use the milk of goats, sheep, camels, and water buffaloes!

Holstein

Jersey

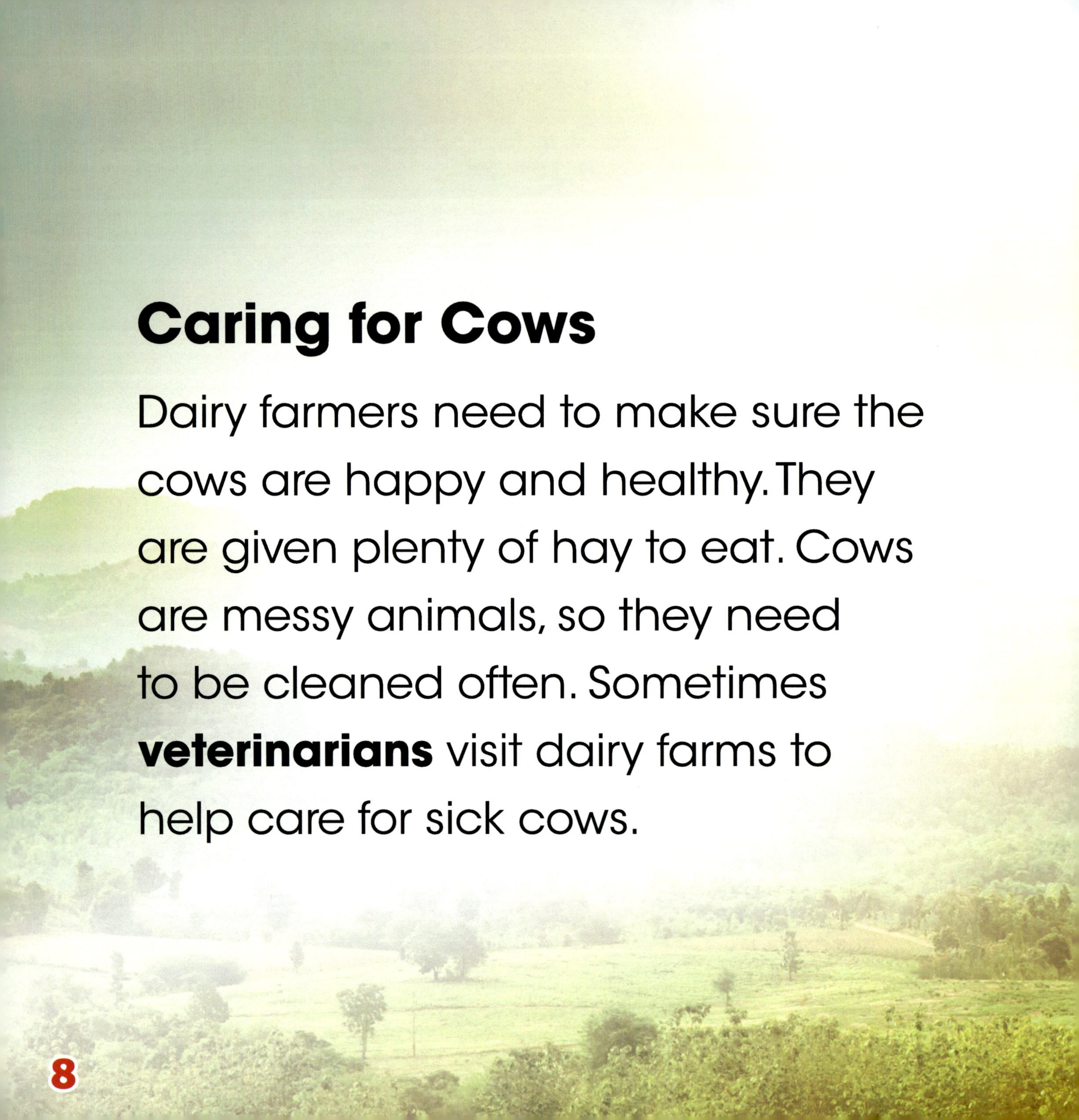

Caring for Cows

Dairy farmers need to make sure the cows are happy and healthy. They are given plenty of hay to eat. Cows are messy animals, so they need to be cleaned often. Sometimes **veterinarians** visit dairy farms to help care for sick cows.

Baby Cows

The cows on dairy farms often have babies. A baby cow is called a calf. Adult cows can't make milk until they have had a calf. When calves become adult cows, they are used to replace older cows that don't make milk any more.

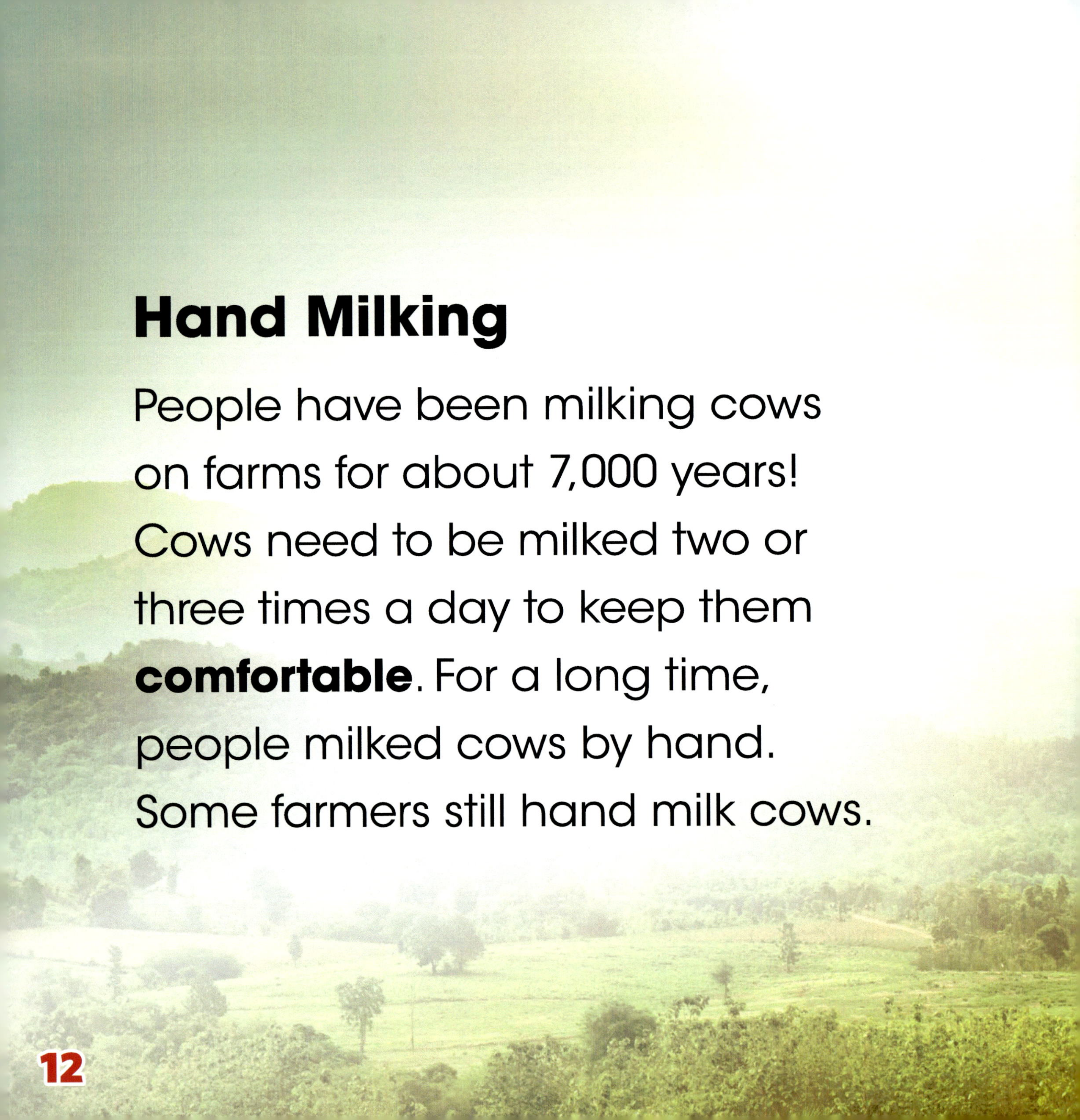

Hand Milking

People have been milking cows on farms for about 7,000 years! Cows need to be milked two or three times a day to keep them **comfortable**. For a long time, people milked cows by hand. Some farmers still hand milk cows.

Machine Milking

Dairy farms today use modern **technology**. Modern dairy farms use machines to milk cows. Milking machines can take milk from all of a cow's **udders** at one time. This saves a lot of time and makes the work quicker.

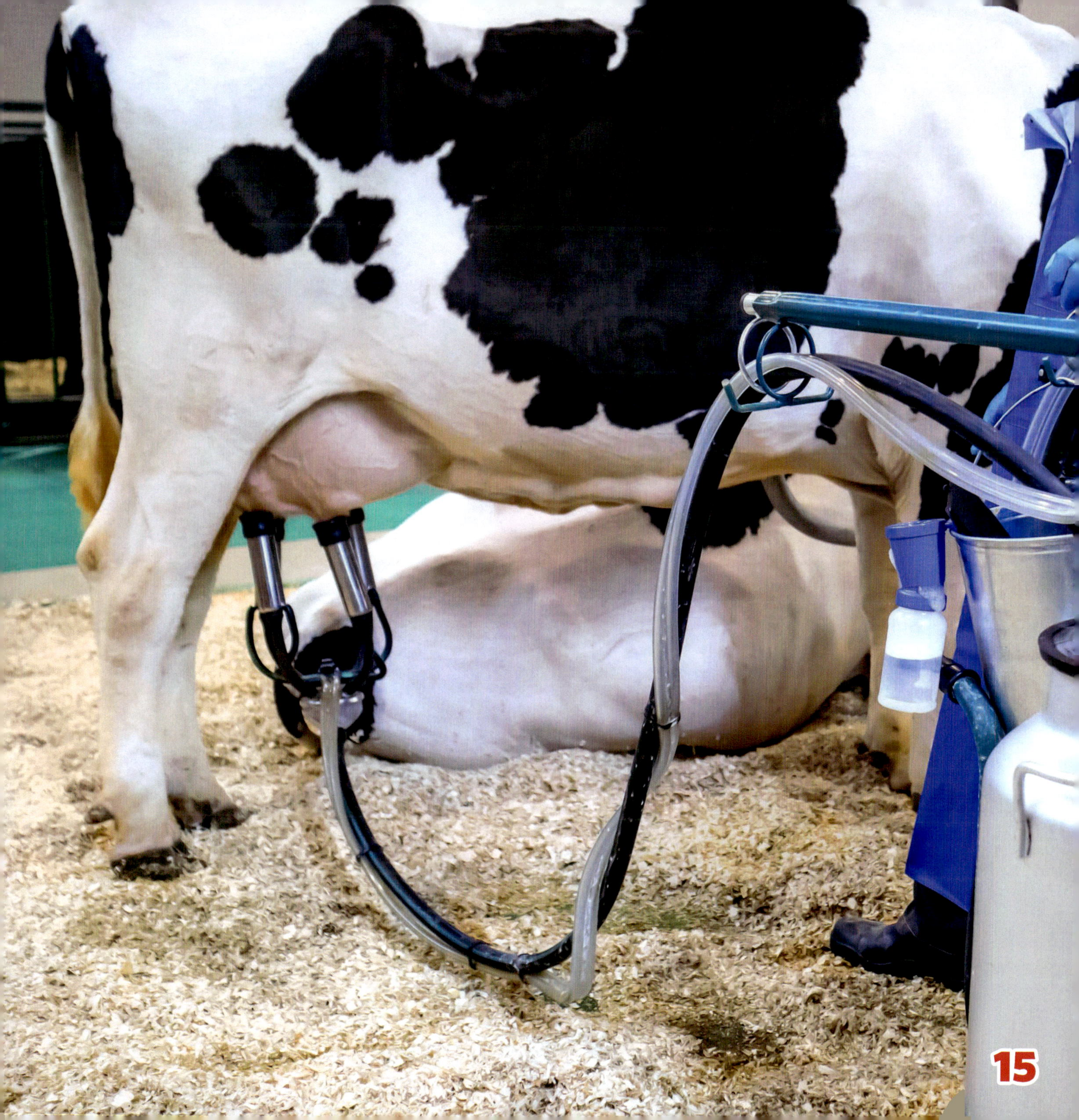

Keeping It Cold

Dairy farmers must store milk properly to avoid making people sick. It's important to keep the milk cold so it doesn't go bad. Modern dairy farms use large **refrigerators** to do this. The trucks that carry milk to factories also use refrigerators.

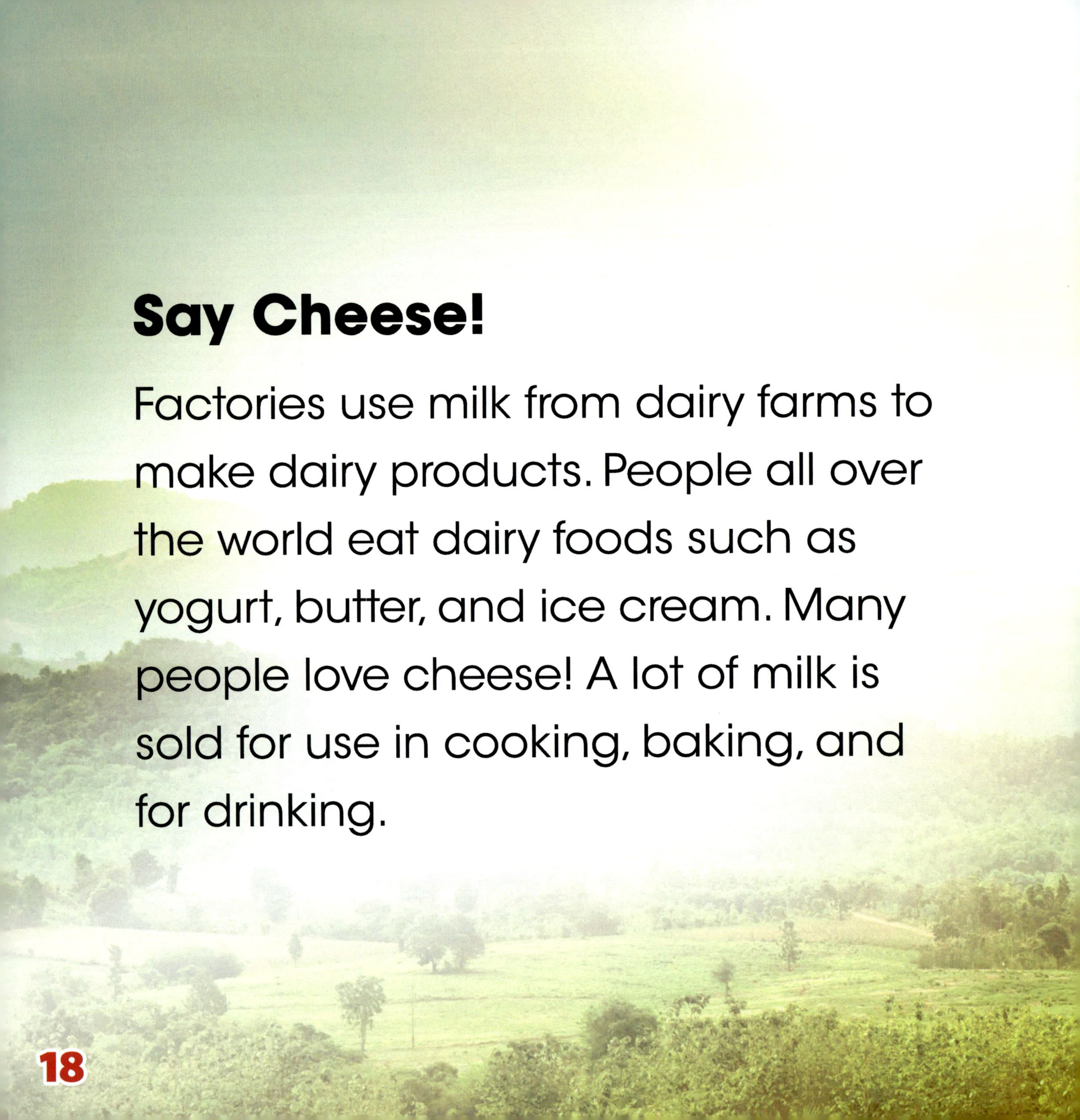

Say Cheese!

Factories use milk from dairy farms to make dairy products. People all over the world eat dairy foods such as yogurt, butter, and ice cream. Many people love cheese! A lot of milk is sold for use in cooking, baking, and for drinking.

Farm Visit

Have you ever visited a dairy farm? You might find cows eating grass in a field. You may see a huge barn with hundreds of cows. Cows are friendly animals. You may even learn how to milk a cow by hand!

GLOSSARY

breed: A kind of animal or plant cared for by people that is different from other forms of the same animal.

comfortable: Feeling at ease and happy.

product: Something that is made and sold to people.

refrigerator: A machine that keeps food cold.

technology: A method that uses science to solve problems and the tools used to solve those problems.

udder: A large, bag-shaped organ that produces milk.

veterinarian: An animal doctor.

FOR FURTHER INFORMATION

WEBSITES

Cows
animalcorner.org/animals/cows/
Learn more about cows and calves at this informative website.

Facts about cows and dairy farms
thefarmerscow.com/dairy-farming-for-kids.php
Read more fun facts about cows and dairy farms.

BOOKS

Hall, Margaret. *Cows and Their Calves*. Mankato, MN: Capstone Press, 2018.

Knutson, Julie. *Cow to Cone*. Ann Arbor, MI: Cherry Lake Publishing, 2019.

Publisher's note to parents and teachers: Our editors have reviewed the websites listed here to make sure they're suitable for students. However, websites may change frequently. Please note that students should always be supervised when they access the internet.

INDEX